Redwork

Devika Girish Sobha

BookLeaf
Publishing

India | USA | UK

Presentation by *BookLeaf Publishing*

Web: www.bookleafpub.com

E-mail: info@bookleafpub.com

ISBN: 9789360949785

First edition 2024

To my Amma, Achan, Hari, the Musketeers,
Sapda and the beautiful souls who helped
me do my redwork

Moving On

Who loves who hates,
The world moves on.
Who gives Who takes,
The world moves on.
Who kills who dies,
The world moves on.
The day dawns, the night draws,
The world moves on.
Who breathes, who stops,
The world moves on.
Summer heat, Autumn falls, Monsoon pours,
Spring flowers, First Snow,
The World moves on.

Some cry, Some laugh,
The World Moves on.
Some win Some lose,
The World moves on.
Some are born, Some die,
The world moves on.
where to begin where to end,
The World moves on.
Celebrational honours, mournful shadows,
The world moves on.

The joy, the smile, the tears, the shrieks, the
shock, the pain, the wonder, the bliss,
The World moves on.

It is the way of the world.
Live in silence.
Live with your peace.
For you are a mere observer.
Your words don't matter,
Your voice, unheard in the chaos.
Be grateful, be thankful. But be silent, enjoy
your blessing. Suffering is the world's way.
Injustice is the world's way.
Let us live our lives in ignorance and leave this
world.
Let us be done with it then.

No.

Stolen Dreams

My breath,
I take in the ashes of the ones who burned
My step,
I walk over the bones of the ones who fought
My voice gets drowned in their cries.
I cry for them, I cry with them, and then the
tears dry up.
The day has come when I feel guilty to breathe,
to move, to speak, to cry, to live.
For I am living a life stolen.
What a time it is, to be a contradiction.
To be an anomaly.
A glitch.
Something to be erased.
Is it not?
For they are me, and I am them.
I with you, you with them, them with you, live a
thousand dreams from our stolen lives.

Girl with the Red Balloon

Of all the colours from the seller's bunch,
The girl chose red.
I wonder why.

Of all the colours from the seller's bunch,
I chose red.
I chose wisely.

Ominous to think of it.
Why, the colour of failure?
Why the colour of violence and blood?

Poetic to think of it.
The colour of love.
The colour of my being.

It is too loud and bold a colour.
The colour for attention
The colour of sin

It is too elegant and warm a colour,
The colour of my beginning.
The colour of my womb

Is she not afraid of the watchful eyes,

The colour that calls for ill,
The colour that calls for death.

Am I not the safest shrouded in red,
The colour of my mother,
And her mother before.

She should let the balloon float away.
Let it burst.
Her wants and greed and sins with it.

I should let the balloon float away.
Let it reach the one after me.
My wants and hopes and prayers with it.

Has her mother not taught her?
Red is not for the good ones.
Has her father not taught her?
Red is for the rebels and the outcasts.
Who does she belong to?
Who lets her run around amuck?

To my mother, who taught me to feel,
To my father, who taught me to think,
To me, to whom I belong,
My being, my thoughts, my words, and my
actions,
I ground it in red.

Hey Stranger, eyeing my red,
Eyeing me,
Crying loud,
I hope you find your red.

Bindings

7

'Let me Out,'
'Let me Out,'
She screamed.
Years of trauma and fear have bound her well
inside me.
For I am afraid,
If she comes out
The world may crumble.

Fear

Who do I fear?
The hands that await me every corner?
The love that is right in front of me,
Beckoning me with open arms?
The caring smudged with thoughts that run wild
across the vicious?
The eyes that don't leave an inch of my body
alone from its scrutiny?
Or are these just my thoughts?
Should I fear myself?
The she inside me?
For she is my world and my world is she.
The walls are cracking and all the hate is seeping
through.
Soaking my bones, her soul.
Fear is everywhere, but what is that I fear?
Who is that I fear?
I don't know.
Maybe I fear for the world.
The endless chaos that it is.

My reality is slipping.
Fear consumes me.
I am pushed into the bottomless pit of despair.
Where should I search for hope?
You tell me.

Reflection

9

I was hurt by the choices of others, I say.
You ask me, what does hurt mean?
The pain in my heart, I say.
What does pain mean, you ask.
The feeling when a star explodes inside you, I
say.
Why does the star explode, you ask.
Because the thoughts build up inside them I say.
Why do the thoughts do so, you ask.
Because I let them, I say.

You look at me and ask, why do you do it to
yourself?
Because I wanted them to accept me, I said.
Don't you want my acceptance, you ask?
I look at you and see my glassy eyes staring
back at me.

You are what you are

Take away the pain
Take away the hurt
Take away the hate
Take away the worry
Take away the regrets
Just leave the pretty stuff.
But then is it you that is left behind?

Happiness

Don't be scared.
I just want to warm myself with your happiness,
I am still searching for mine, you see.
Have you seen it somewhere?
No?
I thought it came your way.
Never mind, I'll keep searching.

Excuse me, have you seen my happiness?
It has the color of Lilac,
No? I thought I would find it here.
You see, I thought it liked places far away.
No worries. I'll keep looking.
Hello there, did you find my happiness in those
books?
It is in the shape of me.
No? Hmmm... I thought it was hiding in the
stories bound here.
Where do I look next?

I have nowhere else to look.
I have asked the music, the sky, the meadows for
my happiness,
Nobody knows where it is.
Should I give up now?

An echo of pain, somewhere inside me.
'I'm here, I'm here.' it cries.
Silence, I say.
Don't you see, I'm searching for my happiness?

Reality

13

Fear not, I don't exist.
I am a figment of my hurt.

Thoughts

They wonder if thoughts could kill.
Oh, but it could.
They couldn't see how the fog smothered me.
They couldn't see the words choking me.
They couldn't see the pain coursing through me.
They couldn't see me struggling for my breath.
These villains, my thoughts,
Twists and turns every memory into
The countless thorns on the vines that bind me.
Carrying me through my past, my present, and
my future,
In the end, leaving me stranded,
Hounded by the worst of the worst in me.

Agony

I opened my body and soul for love.
They filled it with shards of glass,
sewed me up with rough grass, and left me
crawling in the dirt.
It took me an eternity to claw the dirt out of my
being.
A bit more cleansing it needs, and it will be near
perfect.
But the scars remain.

Touch

Is it so bad to be alone?
It is not as if the shadows can hurt you.
The tangible hurts you more.
The touch hurts you more.
It being and its absence.
I prefer the shadows.
At least they leave your body to your own.

Words

17

Words are dripping from my fingertips
Onto your skin.
They leave a mark of who I was with you.
Let those words be with you.
Remember them.
Feel them.
And once I am beyond your touch,
Gather them and cherish them.
Do they hurt you now?
Peel them off.
Burn them.
Gather the ashes and give them to the wind.
They may carry it back to me.

Tumble

I slip and slide
Through the hands of hate.
Tumbling through the river of doubt
A breeze is what it takes,
To push me from the edge
Into the abyss that is my thoughts.

Drowning

The pressure in my chest is building
My breath was losing me
The swishes and swirls of the current dragging
me to the depths
My memories began to ebb to the darkest
corners of my mind,
Or are they leaving me?

I gasp for air,
But the water burns my insides,
My head feels light and full at the same time,
Can it be so?
How long till I die?

One.. two... three...
I can't count anymore,
My limbs tire of the struggle,
The pull of the sea is greater than my will to live
Let it be over quick

The burning...
The pain...
The numbness…
There is nothing else to feel
'Sleep my child,' the shadows are whispering,
I better listen for they await my soul.

Survival

The wounds are still fresh from our last fight,
And yet you have come to pick my bones.
Isn't it enough?
My pain and hurt?
My Damage?
I pass my days praying, for the peace that is yet
to find me.
And when I think I have found it,
You come rushing with your words to shatter the
precious.
Let me live, don't bind me to duty.
Don't keep me caged.
Let me fly. Let me see the skies.
Don't come after me.
Let me survive this life.
You have left enough pain for a lifetime.

The Forgotten

21

In the struggle to reach for the stars,
I forgot to look back at the hands that pushed me
up.
When I ran back to pull them up with me,
All I saw were withered bones and ashes.
What have I done?

Broken Nest

The wind broke our nest.
The river took us with it.
The current took us to the sea.
We are floating in all directions.
I tried to drag you with me.
But you were stubborn, you swam the other way.
I struggled, drowned, came back up, swam, and
am still swimming.
I can see the shore and I call to you.
You blame me for finding it. You blame me for
the horrors.
Why?

You, me, all of us are broken.
We blame everything, You blame me, I blame
fate,
For everything that happened.

But listen to me, birdling,
Nobody is going to drag us to the shore,
So come, swim with me,
Let us find the shore, let us escape the pain.
Let us find our peace.

Origami

23

I want to be origami.
Why?
I can then change the folds and change my
being.

The Smirk

24

My sadness, as it comes out turns back and
smirks.
At least through words, I am let out, it says.

Hide and Seek

Of all your hiding places,
Your favourite remains in my soul.
You say its shadows hide you well,
Is it so?

You keep picking at my walls,
Peeling the layers with your nails.
Is it you who is hiding
Or are you the one seeking?

What is that you hope to find,
Beneath my crumbling walls?
I don't think I have it in me,
What you seek.

Seek elsewhere,
Solace, Peace, Happiness
Whatever is that you are searching for.
I have lost mine a long time ago.

You are scratching at an empty shell.
There is nothing but murky frustration.
Take your hands off before it stains you,
And seek another hiding place

www.ingramcontent.com/pod-product-compliance
Lightning Source LLC
LaVergne TN
LVHW010857200726
843508LV00012B/2922